INDIANA
TRAVEL GUIDE

Unraveling Indiana: A Comprehensive Travel Guide"

BY

Louis L. Powell

TABLE OF CONTENT

My Trip to Indiana: A Journey Through the Heartland

Indiana, a state that had always been on the periphery of my travel radar, surprised me in the most delightful ways. It was a journey through the heartland, where modern cities blended seamlessly with serene countryside, and where history whispered stories of the past at every turn.

As I landed in Indianapolis, the capital city greeted me with open arms. The buzz of the city was infectious, but I couldn't help but be drawn to the iconic Indianapolis Motor Speedway. Standing there, I could almost hear the roar of the engines from the famous Indy 500 races of the past. It was a place where adrenaline and history collided.

My exploration continued as I wandered through downtown Indianapolis, discovering hidden gems like the Soldiers and Sailors Monument on Monument Circle. The city's vibrant arts scene beckoned me, and the Indianapolis Museum of Art, now known as Newfields, revealed a world of creativity and beauty.

But Indiana had more to offer beyond its capital. A scenic drive took me to Bloomington, a college town nestled in lush greenery. There, I strolled through the picturesque campus of Indiana University and found tranquility at the Tibetan Mongolian Buddhist Cultural Center. Nature called, and the Hoosier National Forest offered hiking trails that led to quiet moments of introspection.

French Lick and West Baden Springs were my next stop, where opulent historic hotels transported me back in time. The French Lick Casino added a touch of excitement to my stay, and the whole experience felt like a glamorous retreat.

Brown County, known as the "Little Smokies," was a haven for nature lovers like me. The charming town of Nashville was a treasure trove of art, unique shops, and local cuisine. Hiking in Brown County State Park revealed breathtaking vistas that made me appreciate Indiana's natural beauty.

South Bend and the University of Notre Dame held a different kind of charm. The Basilica of the Sacred Heart and the Studebaker National Museum showcased the intersection of spirituality and innovation.

Finally, my journey culminated at the Indiana Dunes National Park, where the pristine shores of Lake Michigan met towering sand dunes. It was the perfect ending to my adventure, a reminder that Indiana's diverse landscapes were its hidden gems.

Indiana, you've won my heart. Your hospitality, your stories, and your beauty have left an indelible mark. This trip through the heartland was a revelation, and I can't wait to return for more of your captivating surprises.

Introduction: Unraveling Indiana

Welcome to the magnificent state of Indiana! Nestled in the heart of the United States, Indiana is a land of captivating contrasts, blending bustling cities with serene countryside, and history with modernity. This comprehensive travel guide is your key to unlocking the wonders of Indiana, ensuring you make the most of your journey through this fascinating state.

Indiana boasts a rich tapestry of history, culture, and natural beauty. From the iconic Indianapolis Motor Speedway to the picturesque landscapes of Brown County, there is something here for every traveler. Whether you're an adventure seeker, a history enthusiast, a nature lover, or a culinary connoisseur, Indiana will captivate your heart and leave you with cherished memories.

Throughout this guide, we will delve into Indiana's diverse regions and highlight the must-visit attractions and hidden gems. You will also find valuable tips on how to navigate the state, where to savor delicious local cuisines, and which events and festivals to partake in to experience the true essence of Indiana.

So, pack your bags, embark on an unforgettable journey, and let the splendors of Indiana unravel before your eyes. Let's set off on an adventure of a lifetime!

Chapter 1: Introduction to Indiana

Indiana, often referred to as the "Crossroads of America," welcomes travelers with open arms and a warm Midwestern charm. Bordered by the Great Lakes to the north and the Ohio River to the south, this state is steeped in history and boasts a vibrant present.

Geographical Diversity

From the dunes of Lake Michigan to the rolling hills of southern Indiana, the state's geography is as diverse as it is captivating. In the northern region, the Indiana Dunes National Park beckons with its sandy shores, woodlands, and unique biodiversity. Head south, and you'll be enchanted by the scenic beauty of Brown County State Park, a haven for nature enthusiasts.

Historic Significance

Indiana's history is etched into its very fabric. The state played a pivotal role in the westward expansion of the United States, and visitors can explore this heritage at various historical sites and museums. The renowned Conner Prairie allows you to step back in time and experience life in the 19th century, while the Indiana State Museum offers a comprehensive journey through the state's past.

Elkhart - The RV Capital of the World

Elkhart, Indiana, has earned the title of "The RV Capital of the World" for its significant role in the recreational vehicle industry. It is home to numerous manufacturers and suppliers, contributing to the growth of the RV market and the development of innovative and luxurious motorhomes and travel trailers.

Technology and Manufacturing Advancements

Indiana's manufacturing sector has embraced modern technologies, contributing to advancements in various industries. From automotive manufacturers implementing cutting-edge production techniques to pharmaceutical companies pioneering new medical treatments, the state's industrial prowess continues to evolve.

Renewable Energy Initiatives

Indiana has made strides in renewable energy initiatives, including wind and solar power. The state's commitment to green energy is reflected in the development of wind farms and solar energy installations, making significant contributions to the goal of a more sustainable future.

Biomedical Research and Life Sciences

Indiana is home to prominent research institutions and companies in the biomedical and life sciences fields. Advancements in pharmaceuticals, medical devices, and biotechnology have improved healthcare and saved lives around the world.

Innovation Hubs and Startup Ecosystems

Throughout Indiana, innovation hubs and startup ecosystems have flourished, nurturing entrepreneurs and fostering technological advancements. Cities like Indianapolis and Bloomington have become hubs for tech startups, attracting talent and investment to drive innovation.

Infrastructure and Transportation

Indiana's modern infrastructure, including bridges, highways, and public transportation systems, plays a vital role in connecting communities and facilitating economic growth. The state's commitment to maintaining and improving its infrastructure supports commerce and travel.

Higher Education and Research Centers

Indiana's universities and research centers contribute significantly to scientific discovery and technological breakthroughs. Institutions like Indiana University and Notre Dame have fostered research and development in diverse fields, furthering knowledge and pushing the boundaries of innovation.

Embracing the Future

As Indiana embraces the future, the state's modern marvels stand as a testament to its unwavering commitment to progress and innovation. From research and education to manufacturing and renewable energy, Indiana continues to shape the modern world and leave a lasting impact on the realms of science and technology.

Chapter 2: Discovering the Rich History

As you delve deeper into the heart of Indiana, you'll find that history is woven intricately into the fabric of the state. Chapter 2 takes you on a captivating journey through time, unraveling the rich historical tapestry of Indiana.

A Glimpse into the Past

Indiana's history stretches back thousands of years, with evidence of ancient civilizations and Native American cultures that once thrived in the region. The Indiana State Museum is a treasure trove of artifacts and exhibits that showcase the state's prehistoric heritage, offering insight into the lives of the earliest inhabitants.

Pioneering Spirit

The 19th century saw a wave of pioneers and settlers making their way westward, and Indiana played a crucial role in this westward expansion. The iconic covered bridges that dot the landscape harken back to this era, evoking images of horse-drawn carriages and the pioneering spirit that defined the time.

The Underground Railroad

Indiana's location on the border between the North and the South made it a critical junction for the Underground Railroad, a network of secret routes used by enslaved African Americans to escape to freedom in the North. Visitors can explore the Levi Coffin House in

Fountain City, known as the "Grand Central Station" of the Underground Railroad.

Lincoln's Indiana Roots

Before he became the 16th President of the United States, Abraham Lincoln spent much of his childhood in Indiana. The Lincoln Boyhood National Memorial in Lincoln City offers a glimpse into the formative years of this great leader, with a living history farm and informative exhibits.

A Humble Beginnings

Abraham Lincoln was born on February 12, 1809, in a log cabin in Hardin County, Kentucky. However, it was in the rugged wilderness of southern Indiana that he spent much of his childhood and early adolescence. In 1816, when Lincoln was just seven years old, his family moved to Indiana, settling in what is now known as Spencer County.

Life on the Frontier

Indiana was still a frontier state during Lincoln's time, and life was challenging and rugged. The Lincoln family cleared land, built their own cabin, and worked hard to make a living from the land. As a young boy, Lincoln learned the value of hard work, self-reliance, and the importance of education, even though formal schooling was limited.

The Influence of His Mother

Lincoln's mother, Nancy Hanks Lincoln, played a crucial role in shaping his character and instilling in him a love for reading and learning. She encouraged his intellectual curiosity and nurtured his aspirations, planting the seeds of greatness that would one day come to fruition.

The Tragedy of Loss

In 1818, when Lincoln was only nine years old, tragedy struck the family when his mother passed away. Her death had a profound impact on young Abraham, and the loss of his mother left a lasting impression on him throughout his life.

Life Lessons and Values

Growing up in Indiana, Lincoln witnessed the hardships of life on the frontier, and he developed a deep sense of empathy and compassion for others. He saw the struggles of his family and neighbors and learned the importance of fairness, honesty, and perseverance.

Education and Reading

Despite the lack of formal schooling, Lincoln was an avid reader and sought knowledge wherever he could find it. He borrowed books from neighbors and read voraciously, educating himself on a wide range of subjects. His love for reading would stay with him throughout his life and become a defining trait of his intellect.

The Road to Greatness

Lincoln's formative years in Indiana laid the foundation for the character and values that would guide him in his pursuit of greatness. His experiences on the frontier and the lessons he learned from his family and community would shape his leadership style and decision-making as he rose to become the 16th President of the United States.

Commemorating Lincoln's Indiana Roots

Today, visitors can explore the Lincoln Boyhood National Memorial in Lincoln City, Indiana, where a reconstructed cabin and memorial park commemorate Lincoln's time in Indiana. The site offers a glimpse into the early life of the future president and the humble beginnings that would shape the course of American history.

The Industrial Era

Indiana's history is also closely tied to industrial development, particularly in the late 19th and early 20th centuries. Cities like Gary and South Bend played pivotal roles in the steel and automotive industries, contributing significantly to the nation's growth.

Preserving Heritage

Efforts to preserve Indiana's historical sites and landmarks are ongoing, with numerous state parks, museums, and historical societies dedicated to safeguarding the state's heritage. Step inside beautifully restored homes, walk along cobblestone streets, and experience living history demonstrations that breathe life into the past.

Indiana's historical tapestry is diverse, encompassing stories of Native Americans, pioneers, abolitionists, and industrialists. As you explore this chapter, you'll gain a deeper appreciation for the events and figures that shaped Indiana into the state it is today.

Chapter 3: Exploring the Vibrant Cities

Indiana's cities pulse with energy and creativity, offering a delightful mix of urban attractions, cultural experiences, and modern amenities. In Chapter 3, we embark on a tour of the state's vibrant cities, each with its own unique charm.

Indianapolis: The Crossroads of America

The state capital, Indianapolis, is a thriving metropolis that effortlessly blends tradition with innovation. Home to the iconic Indianapolis Motor Speedway, it is a haven for motorsports enthusiasts. The downtown area is a bustling hub of activity, with attractions such as the Indiana

Statehouse, White River State Park, and the Eiteljorg Museum of American Indians and Western Art.

Bloomington: A College Town Gem

Bloomington is more than just a college town; it is a cultural epicenter brimming with creativity. The presence of Indiana University infuses the city with youthful energy, and the lively arts scene embraces music, theater, and visual arts. Nature enthusiasts will relish exploring nearby gems like the Hoosier National Forest and Lake Monroe.

Fort Wayne: Where History and Modernity Meet

Steeped in history, Fort Wayne boasts a charming Old Fort and a rich heritage that you can explore at the Historic Fort Wayne Embassy Theatre. For family-friendly fun, head to the Fort Wayne Children's Zoo, consistently ranked among the best in the nation.

South Bend: Notre Dame and Beyond

South Bend is synonymous with the prestigious University of Notre Dame, and a visit to the campus is a must. The city's vibrant riverfront and burgeoning culinary scene add to its appeal. Don't miss the Studebaker National Museum, which showcases the legacy of the once-prominent automobile manufacturer.

Evansville: Where the Rivers Meet

Nestled along the Ohio River, Evansville offers picturesque river views and a blend of recreational opportunities. The Evansville Museum of Arts, History, and Science is a cultural gem, while the Mesker Park Zoo & Botanic Garden promises a day of family fun.

Lafayette: A Hub of History and Culture

Lafayette boasts a rich history and is the gateway to the Wabash & Erie Canal. History buffs will enjoy a visit to the Tippecanoe Battlefield Museum, while art enthusiasts can explore local galleries and the Art Museum of Greater Lafayette.

Indiana's cities cater to a range of interests, making them perfect destinations for diverse travelers. Whether you're a sports enthusiast, an art lover, a history buff, or a foodie, the cities of Indiana have something extraordinary to offer.

Chapter 4: Journeying Through Natural Wonders

Indiana's natural beauty is a hidden gem waiting to be explored. Chapter 4 takes you on a journey through the state's breathtaking natural wonders, from tranquil lakes to lush forests.

Indiana Dunes National Park

Covering 15,000 acres along the southern shore of Lake Michigan, Indiana Dunes National Park is a paradise for nature lovers. The park's diverse ecosystems include dunes, beaches, forests, wetlands, and prairies. Hike the trails, bask in the sun on the shores of Lake Michigan, and witness stunning sunsets over the water.

A Unique Blend of Nature and History

Indiana Dunes National Park is a place where nature and history intertwine harmoniously. Spanning over 15,000 acres, the park boasts a stunning landscape that includes towering sand dunes, lush forests, serene wetlands, and pristine beaches. It is a sanctuary for a wide array of plant and animal species, making it an ecological gem in the heart of the Midwest.

Majestic Sand Dunes

At the heart of the park are the awe-inspiring sand dunes that rise up to 200 feet above Lake Michigan. These massive dunes were shaped by glaciers thousands of years ago, and they offer panoramic views of the surrounding landscape and the glistening waters of the lake. Climbing the dunes is a favorite activity for visitors seeking a thrilling adventure and a unique perspective on the park's beauty.

Tranquil Beaches

Indiana Dunes National Park boasts 15 miles of pristine beaches along Lake Michigan's shoreline. Visitors can relax on the sandy shores, soak in the sun, and enjoy the cool breeze coming off the lake. Swimming, beachcombing, and beach picnics are popular activities that allow visitors to immerse themselves in the tranquil ambiance of the lakefront.

Rich Biodiversity

The park's diverse ecosystems support an incredible variety of plant and animal life. From rare orchids and carnivorous plants in the wetlands to migratory birds and resident wildlife in the forests, Indiana Dunes is a haven for nature enthusiasts and birdwatchers alike. The park's natural diversity is a testament to the importance of preserving and protecting these unique habitats.

Nature Trails and Exploration

Indiana Dunes National Park offers an extensive network of hiking trails that wind through dunes, forests, and wetlands, providing opportunities for exploration and appreciation of the park's natural wonders. Each trail presents a different perspective of the landscape, and hikers may encounter diverse flora and fauna along the way.

Historical Sites and Cultural Heritage

Beyond its natural beauty, the park is also home to historical sites that offer a glimpse into the region's past. The Chellberg Farm, Bailly Homestead, and the 1933 World's Fair Century of Progress Homes are among the historic treasures that tell the story of human settlement and the cultural heritage of the area.

Conservation and Stewardship

Indiana Dunes National Park is a testament to the value of conservation and stewardship efforts. Over the years, dedicated individuals and organizations have worked tirelessly to protect the park's fragile ecosystems and ensure that future generations can enjoy its natural splendor.

A Place of Inspiration and Recreation

Whether visitors seek solace in the tranquility of the dunes, draw inspiration from the stunning vistas, or partake in recreational activities, Indiana Dunes National Park offers a rejuvenating and enriching experience for all who venture into its embrace.

Brown County State Park

Known as the "Little Smokies" due to its resemblance to the Great Smoky Mountains, Brown County State Park is a haven for outdoor enthusiasts. The park offers hiking, horseback riding, mountain biking, and picturesque vistas from its scenic overlooks.

Clifty Falls State Park

Prepare to be enchanted by the rugged beauty of Clifty Falls State Park. This park is renowned for its stunning waterfalls, including the namesake Clifty Falls, which cascades over limestone cliffs. Explore the deep gorges and scenic trails that wind through the park's diverse landscapes.

Turkey Run State Park

For a taste of Indiana's unique sandstone canyons, head to Turkey Run State Park. The park's rugged terrain is perfect for hiking and exploring, with the opportunity to traverse creek beds and climb ladders to experience its natural wonders up close.

Hoosier National Forest

Encompassing over 200,000 acres, Hoosier National Forest is a vast playground for outdoor adventurers. Discover miles of trails for hiking, horseback riding, and mountain biking. The forest also offers opportunities for camping, fishing, and wildlife viewing.

Chain O' Lakes State Park

Chain O' Lakes State Park is a paradise for water lovers. Its interconnected lakes and waterways offer opportunities for boating, fishing, and kayaking. Explore the scenic channels and enjoy a serene day on the water.

Chapter 5: Indiana's Culinary Delights

Indiana's culinary scene is as diverse as its landscapes. In Chapter 5, we embark on a gastronomic journey, savoring the flavors of the state's signature dishes and farm-to-table delights.

The Hoosier Tenderloin

A true Indiana classic, the Hoosier tenderloin is a must-try delicacy. Indulge in a breaded and fried pork tenderloin sandwich, often served with traditional toppings like lettuce, tomato, and pickles. Each bite is a delightful explosion of flavors and textures.

Sugar Cream Pie

Treat your taste buds to a slice of Indiana's official state pie, the sugar cream pie. With a creamy custard filling and a hint of nutmeg, this indulgent dessert has a rich history dating back to the 1800s.

Farm-to-Table Fare

Indiana's fertile farmlands produce an abundance of fresh produce and locally sourced ingredients. Embrace the farm-to-table movement by dining at restaurants that highlight the best of the season's offerings, from heirloom tomatoes to sweet corn.

Covered Bridge Festival

Experience a step back in time at the Covered Bridge Festival, held annually in Parke County. Celebrate the beauty of the county's historic covered bridges while enjoying arts and crafts, delicious food, and live entertainment.

Feast of the Hunters' Moon

Travel back to the 18th century at the Feast of the Hunters' Moon, a reenactment of the annual fall gathering of the French and Native Americans. Held at Fort Ouiatenon in West Lafayette, this festival showcases colonial-era demonstrations, traditional music, and period-authentic food.

Indiana State Fair

The Indiana State Fair is a summertime tradition that brings together agricultural exhibits, amusement rides, concerts, and mouthwatering fair food. Celebrate the state's farming heritage and enjoy a fun-filled day at the fairgrounds.

Talbot Street Art Fair

For art enthusiasts, the Talbot Street Art Fair in Indianapolis is a premier event. This juried art fair features the works of talented artists from across the country, offering a diverse array of paintings, sculptures, pottery, and more.

Chapter 7: Indiana's Arts and Cultural Scene

Indiana's cultural tapestry is alive and vibrant, with a flourishing arts scene and a wealth of cultural institutions. In Chapter 7, we explore the state's artistic heritage and its thriving arts community.

The Indianapolis Cultural Trail

Embark on a scenic journey along the Indianapolis Cultural Trail, an 8-mile urban pathway that connects neighborhoods, cultural districts, and attractions. Adorned with public art installations, this trail is a celebration of creativity and connectivity.

Eiteljorg Museum of American Indians and Western Art

Discover the beauty and diversity of Native American art and Western landscapes at the Eiteljorg Museum in Indianapolis. The museum's collections and exhibitions offer an enriching perspective on the history and traditions of Native peoples.

Indiana Repertory Theatre

For theater enthusiasts, the Indiana Repertory Theatre in Indianapolis is a cultural gem. The theater stages a variety of productions, from classic plays to contemporary works, offering a captivating theatrical experience.

Richmond Art Museum

Art aficionados will find solace at the Richmond Art Museum, boasting an impressive collection of American art and ceramics. The museum also hosts rotating exhibits featuring regional and national artists.

Fort Wayne Philharmonic

Indulge in the harmonious melodies of the Fort Wayne Philharmonic, a symphony orchestra that offers a diverse repertoire of classical and contemporary performances.

South Bend's First Fridays

Experience the vibrant arts community of South Bend during its First Fridays celebration. On the first Friday of each month, downtown comes alive with art exhibits, live music, and culinary delights.

As you immerse yourself in Indiana's arts and culture, you'll come to appreciate the state's creative spirit and the myriad of ways it manifests in its museums, theaters, galleries, and festivals.

Chapter 8: Unearthing Hidden Gems

Beyond the well-known attractions, Indiana holds a plethora of hidden gems waiting to be discovered. Chapter 8 uncovers some lesser-known yet captivating destinations that are sure to leave a lasting impression.

Marengo Cave

Venture underground and explore the wondrous Marengo Cave, a hidden gem located in southern Indiana. This U.S. National Landmark offers guided tours through stunning underground chambers adorned with unique formations, including stalactites and stalagmites.

West Baden Springs Hotel

Step back in time at the opulent West Baden Springs Hotel, an architectural marvel nestled in the Hoosier National Forest. Known as the "Eighth Wonder of the World" in the early 20th century, this historic hotel boasts a stunning domed atrium and offers a luxurious retreat for visitors.

Tippecanoe River State Park

Find tranquility at Tippecanoe River State Park, a serene haven for nature enthusiasts. The park's winding river, lush forests, and picturesque landscapes make it an ideal spot for hiking, fishing, and canoeing.

Falls of the Ohio State Park

Discover a fossil lover's paradise at Falls of the Ohio State Park, situated along the banks of the Ohio River. This unique park boasts exposed Devonian fossil beds, where visitors can spot ancient fossils dating back millions of years.

Antique Alley

Antique enthusiasts will be delighted by Indiana's Antique Alley, a charming stretch of towns and shops offering a treasure trove of vintage finds. Explore quaint antique stores and flea markets, and you might stumble upon rare collectibles and unique mementos.

DePauw Nature Park

Embrace the tranquility of DePauw Nature Park in Greencastle, a hidden oasis of greenery and hiking trails. The park's scenic beauty, including the impressive 52-foot-tall glacial kame known as the "Big Walnut," provides an excellent escape into nature.

Chapter 9: Adventure and Outdoor Activities

For thrill-seekers and outdoor enthusiasts, Indiana offers an array of adrenaline-pumping activities. Chapter 9 unveils the exciting adventures that await you in the Hoosier State.

Canoeing and Kayaking

Indiana's waterways provide excellent opportunities for canoeing and kayaking. Traverse scenic rivers like the White River, Blue River, and Wabash River, enjoying the picturesque landscapes and wildlife along the way.

Zip Lining and Treetop Adventures

Experience the thrill of zip lining and treetop adventures at various parks and adventure centers throughout the state. Soar through the trees, navigating obstacle courses and suspension bridges for an exhilarating day in the great outdoors.

Dune Sledding

At Indiana Dunes National Park, take part in a unique activity known as dune sledding. Grab a sandboard or sled and slide down the sandy slopes of the towering dunes, providing a dose of excitement and unforgettable memories.

Hot Air Balloon Rides

Take to the skies and enjoy a bird's-eye view of Indiana's beautiful landscapes with a hot air balloon ride. Drift peacefully above rolling hills, forests, and lakes, experiencing the serenity of flight.

ATV and Off-Road Adventures

For off-road enthusiasts, Indiana offers various ATV trails and off-road parks where you can experience the thrill of tearing through rugged terrain and mud bogs.

Caving and Spelunking

Delve into the depths of Indiana's caves and caverns for an exciting spelunking adventure.

Explore hidden passages, underground waterfalls, and fascinating rock formations.

Chapter 10: Pampering Yourself: Luxurious Retreats

Sometimes, the best vacations are about relaxation and pampering. Chapter 10 introduces you to some of Indiana's luxurious retreats and spas where you can indulge in ultimate comfort and rejuvenation.

French Lick Resort

Experience elegance and grandeur at the historic French Lick Resort, nestled amidst the rolling hills of southern Indiana. Pamper yourself with spa treatments, unwind in mineral springs, and enjoy world-class golf courses.

The West Baden Springs Hotel

As mentioned earlier, the West Baden Springs Hotel is not only an architectural marvel but also a luxurious destination offering spa services and opulent accommodations. Treat yourself to a stay in this historic gem.

Serenity Springs

Escape to Serenity Springs, a secluded and romantic resort in Michigan City, Indiana. Stay in cozy cabins with private hot tubs and enjoy a tranquil lakeside setting, perfect for couples seeking a peaceful getaway.

Belterra Casino Resort

Combine luxury and entertainment at Belterra Casino Resort in Florence, Indiana. This resort features a full-service spa, a championship golf course, and a lively casino for those seeking a bit of excitement.

The Conrad Indianapolis

Located in the heart of downtown Indianapolis, The Conrad offers sophisticated accommodations and an award-winning spa. Indulge in rejuvenating treatments and savor exquisite dining experiences.

Westin Indianapolis

Unwind at the Westin Indianapolis, where you can enjoy a range of wellness amenities, including a spa, fitness center, and rooftop pool with panoramic city views.

Chapter 11: Family-Friendly Fun

Indiana is a perfect destination for family vacations, offering a plethora of family-friendly attractions and activities that cater to all ages. Chapter 11 presents a range of exciting adventures that will create cherished memories for the whole family.

Children's Museum of Indianapolis

Prepare for a day of wonder and exploration at the Children's Museum of Indianapolis, the largest children's museum in the world. This interactive museum features numerous exhibits, including Dinosphere, ScienceWorks, and the

Riley Children's Health Sports Legends Experience.

Indianapolis Zoo

Embark on a wild journey at the Indianapolis Zoo, home to over 1,200 animals from around the globe. The zoo's exhibits, such as the Simon Skjodt International Orangutan Center and the Dolphin Pavilion, provide an up-close encounter with a diverse array of wildlife.

Fort Wayne Children's Zoo

Voted one of the nation's top zoos for kids, the Fort Wayne Children's Zoo offers an immersive experience with animals and engaging activities.

Enjoy the African Journey, the Indonesian Rain Forest, and the Australian Adventure zones.

Holiday World & Splashin' Safari

For thrills and spills, head to Holiday World & Splashin' Safari in Santa Claus, Indiana. This family-owned amusement park offers thrilling roller coasters, exciting water slides, and a friendly atmosphere.

Indianapolis Motor Speedway Museum

Introduce your family to the world of racing at the Indianapolis Motor Speedway Museum. Explore the rich history of the iconic

Indianapolis 500 and see historic race cars and memorabilia.

WonderLab Museum of Science, Health & Technology

Located in Bloomington, WonderLab is a hands-on science museum that sparks curiosity and creativity in visitors of all ages. Discover interactive exhibits, live science demonstrations, and educational programs.

Chapter 12: Sports and Recreation

Sports enthusiasts will find plenty to cheer for in Indiana, a state deeply passionate about its athletic heritage. Chapter 12 explores the diverse sports and recreational opportunities that make Indiana a haven for sports lovers.

Indiana Pacers (NBA) and Indiana Fever (WNBA)

Catch an exciting basketball game at Bankers Life Fieldhouse in Indianapolis, home to both the Indiana Pacers and the Indiana Fever. Experience the thrill of NBA and WNBA action with the state's beloved teams.

Indiana Pacers: A Hoosier Tradition

The Indiana Pacers, founded in 1967, have become an integral part of Indiana's sports identity. The team's blue and gold colors symbolize the state's loyalty and pride, and they have been a source of inspiration and excitement for basketball fans across the state for decades.

The Glory Days of the ABA

In the early years, the Pacers were part of the American Basketball Association (ABA), a league known for its fast-paced and innovative style of play. Led by legendary players like Reggie Miller, Mel Daniels, and Roger Brown, the Pacers experienced great success in the

ABA, winning three championships in 1970, 1972, and 1973.

The Transition to the NBA

When the ABA merged with the NBA in 1976, the Pacers made the transition to the bigger stage while maintaining their competitive spirit and passionate fan base. They have continued to be a force to be reckoned with in the NBA, consistently showcasing top-notch talent and earning numerous playoff appearances.

Bankers Life Fieldhouse: The Pacers' Home

Bankers Life Fieldhouse, located in downtown Indianapolis, serves as the proud home of the Indiana Pacers. The state-of-the-art arena provides a vibrant atmosphere for fans to come together and cheer on their team, creating an unforgettable experience for basketball enthusiasts of all ages.

Indiana Fever: Women's Basketball Excellence

The Indiana Fever, founded in 2000, are the WNBA's representation of Indiana's basketball prowess. They have carved their own path of success in women's professional basketball, earning a reputation for their tenacity and skill on the court.

A Championship Triumph

In 2012, the Indiana Fever achieved a remarkable feat by capturing the WNBA Championship. Their journey to the title was marked by resilience and determination, inspiring a new generation of young athletes and showcasing the strength of women's basketball in Indiana.

Empowering Female Athletes

The Indiana Fever have been instrumental in empowering female athletes and fostering opportunities for women in sports. They have become advocates for gender equality in the basketball world, using their platform to drive positive change both on and off the court.

Community Impact

Both the Pacers and the Fever take immense pride in their role as community ambassadors. Through various outreach programs and charitable initiatives, the teams actively engage with fans and give back to the communities that support them.

A Shared Passion

The Indiana Pacers and Indiana Fever embody the passion and dedication that Indiana residents have for basketball. Their impact extends beyond the realm of sports, uniting fans from all walks of life under the common goal of cheering on their teams and celebrating the spirit of competition.

Hoosier Basketball Heritage

As Chapter 15 draws to a close, it reflects on how the Indiana Pacers and Indiana Fever represent the enduring basketball heritage of the Hoosier State. From the iconic moments on the court to the lasting legacy they leave in the hearts of fans, these teams stand as a testament to Indiana's love affair with the game of basketball

Indianapolis Colts (NFL)

For football fans, Lucas Oil Stadium in Indianapolis is where the action unfolds. Join the sea of blue and white to cheer on the Indianapolis Colts as they battle it out on the gridiron.

Minor League Baseball

Indiana boasts several minor league baseball teams, offering an affordable and enjoyable sports experience for families. Head to Victory Field in Indianapolis to watch the Indianapolis Indians, or catch a South Bend Cubs game at Four Winds Field.

Golfing Paradise

Indiana is a golfer's paradise, featuring an abundance of top-notch golf courses designed by renowned architects. Enjoy the picturesque fairways and greens at courses like the Pete Dye Course at French Lick and the Brickyard Crossing Golf Course.

Biking and Hiking Trails

With its varied landscapes, Indiana offers a plethora of biking and hiking trails for outdoor enthusiasts. From the Monon Trail in Indianapolis to the Cardinal Greenway in Muncie, there are paths for every skill level.

Boating and Fishing

Discover Indiana's beautiful lakes and rivers by engaging in boating and fishing adventures. Whether you're into angling or leisurely boating, the state's waterways offer endless opportunities for outdoor recreation.

Chapter 13: A Tour of Wineries and Breweries

Indiana's flourishing wine and craft beer scene has garnered a reputation for producing quality libations. Chapter 13 takes you on a delightful tour of wineries and breweries, where you can savor the flavors of the state.

Indiana Wine Trail

Embark on the Indiana Wine Trail, a delightful journey through the state's picturesque wine country. Visit charming wineries in places like Madison, Nashville, and Bloomington, and indulge in tastings of locally crafted wines.

Oliver Winery and Vineyards

As Indiana's oldest and largest winery, Oliver Winery in Bloomington is a must-visit destination for wine enthusiasts. Enjoy tastings of their award-winning wines and soak in the scenic vineyard views.

Upland Brewing Company

Founded in Bloomington, Upland Brewing Company has become a staple in Indiana's craft beer scene. Sample a wide selection of handcrafted brews, ranging from classic ales to experimental beers.

Sun King Brewery

Head to Indianapolis to experience Sun King Brewery, a beloved local brewery known for its innovative beers and commitment to sustainability. Enjoy a tasting flight and see why Sun King is a favorite among Hoosiers.

Traders Point Creamery

For a unique experience, visit Traders Point Creamery in Zionsville, where organic dairy products and craft beers converge. Explore the creamery's farmstead and enjoy a farm-to-table meal with a cold pint.

Indiana Distilleries

Indiana's craft beverage scene extends to spirits as well. Visit one of the state's distilleries to sample loA Booming Craft Spirits Scene

In recent years, Indiana has witnessed a boom in craft distilleries, each with its unique approach to spirit-making. From small-batch bourbons to handcrafted gins and artisanal vodkas, these distilleries take pride in sourcing local ingredients and producing spirits with a distinct Hoosier flavor.

Embracing Indiana's Agricultural Heritage

Many Indiana distilleries embrace the state's agricultural heritage by using locally grown grains and botanicals in their recipes. This commitment to sourcing locally not only supports local farmers but also ensures that the spirits truly capture the essence of Indiana's terroir.

Bourbon and Beyond

Bourbon, with its deep roots in American history, takes center stage in Indiana's distilleries. The state's fertile soil and favorable climate provide the perfect conditions for growing the corn that forms the backbone of this beloved spirit. Craft bourbon makers pay homage to tradition while infusing their own innovative twists, resulting in a diverse and exciting range of expressions.

Artisanal Gins

Indiana's craft distillers are also reviving the art of gin-making with a focus on botanicals and unique flavor profiles. Juniper berries, along with a medley of local and exotic botanicals, are carefully balanced to create gins that cater to both classic cocktail enthusiasts and those seeking adventurous sipping experiences.

Hoosier-Infused Vodkas

Vodka, a versatile and popular spirit, is not left behind in Indiana's distillery scene. Some craft distillers take it a step further by infusing their vodkas with locally sourced fruits, herbs, and spices, adding a distinctive Hoosier twist to this global favorite.

Award-Winning Whiskeys

Indiana distilleries have garnered recognition and acclaim for their exceptional whiskeys. Whether it's the smoothness of their ryes, the complexity of their single malts, or the character of their blended whiskeys, these craft distillers are putting Indiana on the map as a destination for whiskey connoisseurs.

Tasting Rooms and Experiences

Visiting Indiana distilleries is not just about savoring spirits; it's also about experiencing the artistry and craftsmanship firsthand. Many distilleries offer tasting rooms where guests can sample their creations, learn about the distillation process, and even meet the master distillers who pour their passion into every bottle.

A Sense of Community

Beyond the spirits themselves, Indiana's craft distillery scene fosters a sense of community and camaraderie. Distillers often collaborate, share knowledge, and support each other, creating a tight-knit network of artisans dedicated to elevating the craft of distillation in the Hoosier State.

Preserving Tradition, Embracing Innovation

Indiana distilleries embody the spirit of the state itself—where tradition and innovation coexist harmoniously. Rooted in the past and looking toward the future, these distilleries are leaving their mark on the world of spirits and proudly showcasing the flavor and character of Indiana with each carefully crafted sip.

Chapter 14: Road Tripping Across Indiana

Embark on an unforgettable road trip across Indiana, where scenic byways and charming towns beckon travelers to explore the state's hidden gems. Chapter 14 presents some of the most scenic routes and must-visit destinations for a road trip adventure.

Indiana State Road 135

Indiana State Road 135: A Scenic Drive Through the Heart of Indiana

Connecting North and South

Indiana State Road 135, also known as SR 135, spans approximately 88 miles, running north to south through the heart of the Hoosier State. As you traverse this scenic route, you'll witness the diverse landscapes that Indiana has to offer, from rolling hills and lush farmlands to picturesque forests and meandering streams.

Brown County Beauty

One of the highlights of SR 135 is its passage through the stunning Brown County, often referred to as the "Little Smokies of Indiana." The drive through this region is a treat for the eyes, especially during the fall season when the foliage bursts into a breathtaking array of colors.

Charming Towns and Villages

Along SR 135, you'll encounter a series of charming towns and villages, each with its own unique character and local attractions. Explore Nashville, a renowned artist community where galleries, craft shops, and quaint eateries beckon visitors. Discover Story, an enchanting village that seems frozen in time, offering a glimpse of Indiana's past.

Outdoor Adventures

Indiana's natural beauty is on full display along SR 135, inviting outdoor enthusiasts to partake in various recreational activities. Hiking trails, fishing spots, and nature preserves dot the landscape, providing opportunities to connect with nature and indulge in outdoor adventures.

State Parks and Forests

As you journey along SR 135, you'll pass near several of Indiana's state parks and forests. Take a detour to explore destinations like Brown County State Park, where you can hike, bike, and admire the scenic vistas from the park's scenic overlooks.

Quaint Inns and Lodges

For those seeking a leisurely and relaxed experience, SR 135 offers a selection of charming inns and lodges where you can unwind and enjoy the serenity of the countryside. These accommodations provide the perfect setting to escape the bustle of everyday life and immerse yourself in the beauty of Indiana's rural landscapes.

Historic Landmarks

The road is not without its historical significance. Along SR 135, you'll encounter historic landmarks that offer a glimpse into Indiana's past. Explore local museums and historical sites to learn about the region's heritage and the people who shaped its history.

Embracing the Scenic Drive

As you travel along Indiana State Road 135, you'll find that the journey itself becomes a destination. Embrace the beauty of the changing landscapes, the allure of charming towns, and the tranquility of nature as you savor every moment of this scenic drive through the heart of Indiana.

Known as the "Hills of Brown," Indiana State Road 135 takes you through the stunning landscapes of Brown County. Wind your way through rolling hills, dense forests, and picturesque farmlands, making stops in quaint towns like Nashville and Story.

Ohio River Scenic Byway

Ohio River Scenic Byway: A Serene Journey along the Mighty River

Following the Ohio River

The Ohio River Scenic Byway traces the course of the mighty Ohio River, which served as a lifeline for exploration and settlement in the early days of America. As you drive along this scenic route, you'll be enchanted by the river's gentle flow and the stories it carries of the nation's past.

Riverfront Parks and Scenic Overlooks

The byway is dotted with riverfront parks and scenic overlooks, offering perfect vantage points to behold the tranquil beauty of the Ohio River. Take a moment to immerse yourself in the serene atmosphere and enjoy breathtaking views of the river and the surrounding landscapes.

Historic River Towns

The Ohio River Scenic Byway meanders through a series of historic river towns, each with its own distinctive character and rich heritage. Stop in these charming towns to explore their historic districts, visit local museums, and discover the tales of early settlers and the industries that once thrived along the riverbanks.

River Activities and Recreation

The Ohio River invites exploration beyond the byway. Engage in recreational activities such as boating, fishing, and birdwatching, allowing you to connect with the river's natural splendor and abundant wildlife. Seek out marinas and boat launches for a chance to embark on your own river adventure.

The Influence of River Trade

The Ohio River has long been a vital artery for trade and commerce. Learn about its significance in transporting goods and connecting communities during the heyday of riverboats and steamships. Explore museums and exhibits that shed light on the river's role in shaping the economy and culture of the region.

Historic Bridges

The Ohio River is spanned by numerous historic bridges, each a testament to engineering ingenuity and architectural beauty. Marvel at the iconic truss structures that cross the river, connecting states and fostering the flow of people and ideas.

Riverfront Festivals and Events

Throughout the year, the river towns along the Ohio River Scenic Byway come alive with festivals and events that celebrate the river's cultural heritage. Experience the warmth of local hospitality, sample regional cuisine, and join in the festivities that unite communities along the riverbanks.

A Journey of Serenity

As you journey along the Ohio River Scenic Byway, you'll be enveloped in a sense of serenity and tranquility. The river's timeless flow and the picturesque landscapes will leave a lasting impression, calling you back to embrace the peace and beauty of this majestic waterway.

Following the course of the majestic Ohio River, this scenic byway offers breathtaking river views and a glimpse into Indiana's river towns. From Jeffersonville to Lawrenceburg, enjoy historic sites, charming riverfront parks, and riverboat cruises.

The Historic National Road

The Historic National Road: Tracing the Path of America's First Highway

A Road of Historic Significance

The Historic National Road, also known as the Cumberland Road, holds a special place in American history. Authorized by President Thomas Jefferson in 1806, this pioneering highway was the first major public works project funded by the federal government. It served as a crucial gateway to the west, promoting westward expansion and facilitating commerce, migration, and communication across the young nation.

Traversing through Six States

Stretching over 600 miles, the Historic National Road spans through six states, starting from Cumberland, Maryland, and concluding in Vandalia, Illinois. As you journey along this historic route, you'll pass through Maryland, Pennsylvania, West Virginia, Ohio, Indiana, and

Illinois, each segment offering its own unique blend of historical landmarks and scenic vistas.

Landmarks of the Past

Along the Historic National Road, you'll encounter a myriad of historical landmarks that harken back to the early days of American expansion. Explore former stagecoach inns and taverns that provided rest and refreshments to weary travelers, as well as preserved tollhouses that remind us of the early system of funding and maintaining the road.

Visit historical sites such as Fort Necessity in Pennsylvania, where a young George Washington experienced his first military defeat, and the Wheeling Suspension Bridge in West Virginia, an engineering marvel of its time.

Quaint Towns and Charming Communities

As you journey along the Historic National Road, you'll have the opportunity to explore charming towns and communities that have thrived along the route for centuries. Experience the warmth of small-town hospitality, browse antique shops, and savor local cuisines that celebrate the region's rich cultural heritage.

Embracing the Scenic Beauty

The Historic National Road meanders through diverse landscapes, ranging from rolling hills and scenic farmlands to rugged mountains and serene rivers. The journey offers panoramic views of the countryside, allowing you to immerse yourself in the natural beauty that has drawn travelers to this historic route for generations.

A Road of Reflection

The Historic National Road stands as a road of reflection, offering a glimpse into the challenges, triumphs, and aspirations of the early pioneers who traveled its path. As you traverse this historic route, you'll gain a deeper appreciation for the resilience and determination that shaped America's westward expansion and forged the nation's identity.

Preserving History

Efforts to preserve and protect the Historic National Road continue to this day. The road's historical significance is celebrated through interpretive centers, museums, and preservation societies that ensure its legacy is safeguarded for future generations.

As you journey along the Historic National Road, you'll be reminded of the indomitable spirit of exploration that defined America's past. Each mile you travel becomes a tribute to the pioneers who paved the way for the nation's growth and a celebration of the road's enduring place in American history.

Step back in time along the Historic National Road, which was once a vital route for westward expansion. This road trip takes you through Terre Haute, Richmond, and other towns with fascinating history and well-preserved landmarks.

Indiana's Covered Bridges

Indiana's Covered Bridges: Relics of Nostalgia and Engineering Marvels

A Journey through Time

Indiana's covered bridges transport you to a bygone era, evoking images of horse-drawn carriages, dusty country roads, and the spirit of exploration. Travel along scenic routes that lead you to these iconic landmarks, which have withstood the test of time and weathered the changing landscapes.

Historic Landmarks

Each covered bridge in Indiana tells a unique story of the communities it has served and the lives it has touched. From the historic Bridgeton Covered Bridge, built in 1868 and beautifully restored after a devastating fire, to the Medora Covered Bridge, one of Indiana's oldest surviving covered bridges, these structures are symbols of the state's heritage and enduring spirit.

Architectural Marvels

While Indiana's covered bridges exude rustic charm, they are also engineering marvels. The intricate truss systems and designs showcase the ingenuity of early bridge builders who crafted these structures to withstand the forces of nature. Take a moment to admire the craftsmanship and attention to detail that have allowed these bridges to stand strong for generations.

Scenic Beauty

The covered bridges of Indiana are often nestled amidst scenic landscapes, creating a picture-perfect setting for photographers and nature enthusiasts. Surrounded by rolling hills, winding rivers, and lush greenery, these bridges offer a timeless and serene backdrop for unforgettable moments.

Covered Bridge Festivals

Celebrate the legacy of Indiana's covered bridges at one of the many covered bridge festivals held throughout the state. These lively events feature arts and crafts, live music, delicious food, and, of course, the chance to explore and learn about these historic structures up close.

Embracing the Nostalgia

As you traverse the countryside and encounter these covered bridges, you'll feel a sense of nostalgia for a simpler time. The creaking wooden floors, the sight of sunlight filtering through the roof, and the echo of hooves on the planks evoke a longing for a past filled with quaint charm and unhurried moments.

Preserving Heritage

Preserving Indiana's covered bridges is an ongoing effort that involves local communities, historians, and bridge enthusiasts. By visiting these bridges and learning about their history, you become a part of the collective effort to safeguard these architectural treasures for future generations to appreciate and enjoy.

Timeless Beauty and Enduring Spirit

Indiana's covered bridges embody the timeless beauty of a bygone era and the enduring spirit of the communities they represent. As you traverse the countryside and cross these historic structures, you'll feel a connection to Indiana's past, a reverence for its heritage, and an appreciation for the craftsmanship that has made these bridges an integral part of the state's identity.

Embark on a road trip to explore Indiana's iconic covered bridges. Start in Parke County, known as the "Covered Bridge Capital of the World," and meander through the countryside to discover these picturesque structures.

Indiana's Wine and Waterfalls Trail

Indiana's Wine and Waterfalls Trail: A Scenic and Enchanting Journey

Chasing Waterfalls

The Wine and Waterfalls Trail takes you through some of Indiana's most picturesque landscapes, where waterfalls cascade amidst lush greenery. Begin your journey by exploring the breathtaking waterfalls, such as Cataract Falls, McCormick's Creek Falls, and Williamsport Falls. Each waterfall offers a serene and awe-inspiring backdrop, perfect for capturing moments of tranquility in the midst of nature's beauty.

Exploring Wineries

Indiana's wine country is a hidden gem, boasting an array of wineries that produce exceptional wines. As you venture along the trail, visit renowned wineries like Oliver Winery, Huber's Orchard, Winery & Vineyards, and Butler Winery. Delight in wine tastings that showcase a diverse selection of varietals, from robust reds to crisp whites, each with a unique character that reflects the state's terroir.

Scenic Vineyard Views

The wineries along the Wine and Waterfalls Trail often boast picturesque vineyard views. Take a leisurely stroll through the vineyards, where rows of grapevines stretch as far as the eye can see. Breathe in the fresh air and relish the scenic beauty of the countryside, creating the perfect ambiance for a relaxing wine-tasting experience.

Wine and Food Pairings

Pairing Indiana wines with delectable dishes is an integral part of the trail experience. Indulge in the art of wine and food pairing as you savor gourmet meals at winery restaurants, featuring locally sourced ingredients that complement the flavors of the wines. From charcuterie boards to farm-to-table delicacies, each dish enhances the tasting experience, creating a symphony of flavors.

Charming Towns and Artisanal Shops

The Wine and Waterfalls Trail takes you through charming towns that offer more than just wineries and waterfalls. Explore Bloomington, known for its vibrant arts scene and eclectic shops. Discover Nashville, an enchanting artist's haven where you can find unique handmade crafts and artwork.

Capturing Unforgettable Moments

Throughout the Wine and Waterfalls Trail, you'll find numerous opportunities to capture unforgettable moments. Whether it's a romantic sunset over the vineyards, the cascading waters of a waterfall, or the laughter shared during a wine tasting with friends, each memory will become a cherished part of your journey.

Supporting Local Businesses

By embarking on the Wine and Waterfalls Trail, you support local wineries, restaurants, and businesses that contribute to Indiana's thriving wine industry. Your appreciation for the state's natural wonders and love for its wines make you a part of the community that celebrates the essence of Indiana.

Combine the joy of wine tasting with the beauty of waterfalls on this scenic road trip. Explore wineries in southern Indiana, such as Brown County and Bloomington, and make detours to visit stunning waterfalls like McCormick's Creek Falls and Cataract Falls.

Indiana's Amish Country Loop

Indiana's Amish Country Loop: A Journey Through Timeless Tradition

Discovering Amish Culture

Embark on a journey to uncover the unique culture and traditions of the Amish community in Indiana. As you traverse the Amish Country Loop, you'll encounter horse-drawn buggies traveling along country roads, witness Amish farmers tending to their fields, and observe artisans crafting handmade goods.

Quaint Amish Towns

The Amish Country Loop takes you through quaint towns that exude charm and simplicity. Explore Shipshewana, known for its bustling flea market and authentic Amish experiences. Stroll through Middlebury, where Amish-owned shops offer handmade furniture and traditional crafts. Delight in the peaceful ambiance of Nappanee, where the Amish way of life thrives.

Handcrafted Amish Goods

In the heart of Amish Country, you'll find a treasure trove of handcrafted goods. Visit the workshops and stores to discover exquisite quilts, meticulously crafted furniture, handmade baskets, and other traditional crafts. Each piece carries the hallmark of Amish craftsmanship—meticulous attention to detail and a commitment to quality.

Amish Country Cooking

Savor the flavors of Amish Country with authentic home-cooked meals. Dine at family-owned restaurants and bakeries, where recipes passed down through generations offer hearty comfort food. Indulge in mouthwatering fried chicken, homemade noodles, freshly baked bread, and mouthwatering pies that will leave a lasting impression on your taste buds.

Experiencing Simplicity

In Amish Country, you'll experience a way of life rooted in simplicity and community. Take in the serene landscapes, where golden fields stretch to the horizon, and horse-drawn buggies share the road with modern vehicles. Amish families working together in their farms and children playing in the yards exemplify the strong bonds of community that define the Amish way of life.

Amish Country Markets

As you explore the Amish Country Loop, be sure to visit the bustling markets where you can find an array of fresh produce, homemade goods, and local crafts. From seasonal fruits and vegetables to handwoven baskets and jars of preserves, these markets offer a glimpse into the self-sufficiency and resourcefulness of the Amish community.

Embracing the Amish Spirit

As you traverse Indiana's Amish Country Loop, you'll be immersed in the essence of a way of life that cherishes simplicity, community, and tradition. The timeless traditions, the warm hospitality, and the dedication to craftsmanship will leave a lasting impression on your heart,

drawing you closer to the enduring spirit of the Amish people.

Experience the charm of Amish Country on a road trip through northern Indiana. Visit Shipshewana, Nappanee, and Middlebury, where you can sample homemade Amish goods, explore handcrafted furniture shops, and take in the serene countryside.

Chapter 15: Memorable Souvenirs and Keepsakes

Handcrafted Artwork

Handcrafted Artwork: Celebrating Indiana's Artistic Spirit

Indiana is a haven for art enthusiasts, boasting a rich tradition of craftsmanship and creativity. Chapter 15 delves deeper into the world of handcrafted artwork, where the talents of local artists come to life, capturing the essence of the Hoosier State.

Painting Indiana's Landscapes

Immerse yourself in the beauty of Indiana's landscapes through captivating paintings created by talented artists. From serene rural scenes and rolling farmlands to picturesque lakes and charming towns, these artworks showcase the diversity and natural charm of the state. Whether you prefer realistic depictions or abstract interpretations, the paintings will bring a touch of Indiana's scenic wonder into your living space.

Pottery: Artistry in Clay

Indiana's pottery scene is a treasure trove of creativity, with artists shaping clay into stunning pieces of functional and decorative art. Delight in handcrafted pottery, featuring unique glazes, textures, and designs inspired by Indiana's flora, fauna, and cultural heritage. From delicate vases and graceful bowls to intricate sculptures, each pottery piece is a testament to the artist's skill and passion.

Sculpting Indiana's Culture

Capture the soul of Indiana's culture through finely sculpted artwork. Skilled artisans bring to life historical figures, iconic landmarks, and symbolic representations of the state's heritage. These sculptures embody the essence of Indiana's people and history, evoking a sense of pride and admiration for the Hoosier State.

Woodcraft: Nature's Beauty Preserved

Discover the artistry of woodworking, where talented craftsmen transform wood into exquisite creations. From intricate furniture and finely carved figurines to handcrafted jewelry boxes and cutting boards, each piece tells a story of skilled craftsmanship and an appreciation for the natural beauty of Indiana's forests.

Glassblowing: Art in the Flame

Witness the mesmerizing art of glassblowing, where skilled artists manipulate molten glass into delicate and vibrant masterpieces. From colorful glass vases and shimmering ornaments to intricate paperweights and awe-inspiring sculptures, these pieces represent the magic of artistic expression and the play of light.

Fiber Arts: Weaving Stories

Explore the world of fiber arts, where skilled artisans weave stories into textiles. From handwoven rugs and vibrant tapestries to intricately embroidered wall hangings and cozy quilts, these textile creations infuse warmth and artistry into any living space, celebrating Indiana's rich traditions and creative spirit.

Whether you choose to adorn your home with paintings, pottery, sculptures, woodcrafts, glassblowing, or fiber arts, these handcrafted artworks will not only add beauty to your surroundings but also serve as a tangible connection to Indiana's artistic heritage. Each piece is a testament to the passion, skill, and imagination of the artists who call Indiana home.

As you cherish these handcrafted treasures, may they remind you of the artistry that permeates every corner of the Hoosier State, and may they inspire you to explore and support the creative community wherever your journey takes you.

Hoosier Apparel and Merchandise

Hoosier Apparel and Merchandise: Wear Your Indiana Pride

Hoosier T-Shirts and Hoodies
One of the most popular ways to display your love for Indiana is through Hoosier-themed T-shirts and hoodies. These garments come in a variety of designs, colors, and styles, making it easy to find the perfect one that resonates with your sense of fashion. Whether you opt for a classic "Hoosier" logo or a creative graphic representing Indiana's iconic landmarks, wearing these T-shirts and hoodies will instantly connect you with the state's unique identity.

Stylish Hats and Caps
Top off your outfit with a stylish Hoosier hat or cap, providing both a fashionable accessory and a nod to Indiana's heritage. From baseball caps featuring the state's name to trendy trucker hats displaying "Hoosier" in bold letters, these

headwear options are a fun way to proudly show off your Indiana roots.

Cozy Sweatshirts and Jackets

Stay warm and cozy during colder months with Hoosier-themed sweatshirts and jackets. Embroidered or printed with Indiana motifs, these comfortable garments allow you to stay snug while spreading your love for the Hoosier State.

Indiana-Inspired Accessories

Beyond clothing, a plethora of Indiana-inspired accessories awaits you. From scarves and gloves in Indiana's colors to wristbands with Hoosier logos, these accessories offer subtle ways to incorporate your Indiana pride into your daily wardrobe.

Sports Team Merchandise

For sports enthusiasts, donning apparel and merchandise representing Indiana's beloved sports teams is a must. Whether it's cheering on the Indiana Pacers in NBA or supporting the

Indianapolis Colts in NFL, showing loyalty to these teams fosters a sense of community and camaraderie among Hoosier fans.

Home Decor and Souvenirs
Carry the Hoosier spirit into your living space with home decor and souvenirs. Hoosier-themed wall art, throw pillows, coffee mugs, and keychains add a touch of Indiana charm to your home and make for thoughtful gifts for friends and family.

Customized Hoosier Merchandise
For a personal touch, consider customizing Hoosier merchandise with your name or initials. Customized apparel and accessories add a unique flair to your collection, making them one-of-a-kind keepsakes of your Indiana adventures.

Wearing Hoosier apparel and using Indiana-themed merchandise is not just a display of state pride but also a way to connect with fellow Hoosiers, no matter where your travels take you. As you carry these tokens of Indiana with you, they will become cherished reminders of the welcoming spirit and strong sense of community that define the Hoosier State.

Embrace your inner Hoosier by purchasing apparel and merchandise emblazoned with the iconic "Hoosier" nickname. From T-shirts to hats, proudly display your Indiana pride.

Amish Quilts and Crafts

Amish Quilts and Crafts: A Tapestry of Tradition and Craftsmanship

Amish Quilts: Stitching Stories

Amish quilts are renowned for their exquisite craftsmanship and intricate designs, each stitch a labor of love. Traditionally made by hand, these quilts often feature geometric patterns, bold colors, and precise stitching. Every quilt is a masterpiece, reflecting the individual creativity of the quilter and the collective heritage of the Amish community.

These quilts not only adorn beds and walls but also hold stories of tradition, faith, and community. Passed down as heirlooms, Amish quilts symbolize warmth, comfort, and the enduring spirit of the Amish way of life.

Handcrafted Wooden Furniture

In addition to quilts, the Amish are renowned for their exceptional handcrafted wooden furniture.

With a focus on quality and craftsmanship, each piece is meticulously crafted using traditional woodworking techniques. From solid oak dining tables to finely carved rocking chairs, Amish furniture showcases the beauty of natural wood and the skill of the artisans.

Amish furniture is more than just functional; it embodies the simplicity, durability, and timelessness of Amish lifestyle and values. These pieces are built to last for generations, carrying with them the legacy of skilled craftsmanship and a commitment to sustainability.

Handwoven Baskets and Crafts

Amish artisans also excel in the art of basket weaving and crafting. Handwoven baskets, made from materials such as reed, willow, and splint, are not only practical for storage but also display a delicate beauty. Each basket is a reflection of the weaver's expertise and a dedication to preserving the traditional techniques.

Alongside baskets, Amish crafts encompass a wide range of creations, including handmade toys, decorative pieces, and functional items. These crafts exemplify the art of simplicity and the joy of creating something beautiful from the most basic of materials.

Quilt and Craft Shows

To truly appreciate the artistry of Amish quilts and crafts, consider visiting one of the many quilt and craft shows in Indiana. These events provide an opportunity to meet the artisans, learn about their techniques, and purchase authentic, handcrafted creations directly from the makers.

Supporting the Amish Community

By investing in Amish quilts and crafts, you not only bring home treasured pieces of art but also support the Amish community's way of life. The income from their craftsmanship helps sustain their traditional lifestyle, allowing them to continue creating these exceptional works of art.

As you immerse yourself in the world of Amish quilts and crafts, you'll find more than just beautifully crafted items; you'll discover a connection to a community deeply rooted in tradition, values, and the love of creating things by hand.

Explore the Amish markets and shops to find exquisite quilts and handcrafted crafts. Amish quilts, with their intricate designs and meticulous craftsmanship, make for cherished heirlooms.

Local Food and Beverages:

Local Food and Beverages: Savoring Indiana's Culinary Delights

Farm-to-Table Cuisine

Indiana takes pride in its farm-to-table movement, where restaurants and eateries embrace locally sourced ingredients to craft mouthwatering dishes. Indulge in the freshest produce, meats, and dairy products sourced from nearby farms, ensuring that each bite is a celebration of the region's agricultural bounty.

Treat yourself to dishes like tender Indiana-raised beef, savory pork prepared with traditional recipes, and seasonal vegetables that reflect the changing landscape of the Hoosier State. The farm-to-table ethos not only supports local farmers but also showcases the rich flavors and quality of Indiana's natural produce.

Iconic Hoosier Fare

No exploration of Indiana's culinary scene is complete without trying some iconic Hoosier fare. Delight in breaded tenderloin sandwiches, a Hoosier specialty known for its generous size and crunchy exterior. Savor sugar cream pie, the official state pie of Indiana, with its creamy custard filling and dusting of cinnamon.

For a taste of the state's German heritage, try hearty sausages, sauerkraut, and homemade noodles. Each bite tells a story of Indiana's diverse cultural influences and the cherished recipes passed down through generations.

Craft Breweries and Wineries

Indiana's craft beer and wine scene has flourished in recent years, with a wide array of breweries and wineries offering unique libations. Embark on a tasting journey to savor handcrafted beers that range from hoppy IPAs to smooth stouts, all brewed with passion and creativity.

For wine enthusiasts, Indiana's wineries produce an impressive selection of varietals, including robust reds and crisp whites. Sip on award-winning wines, taking in the flavors that are shaped by the state's distinct terroir.

Artisanal Chocolates and Treats

For those with a sweet tooth, Indiana's artisanal chocolates and treats are a delight to savor. Discover locally made chocolates infused with inventive flavors, handcrafted caramels that melt in your mouth, and nostalgic candies that evoke memories of simpler times.

Food Festivals and Markets

To fully immerse yourself in Indiana's culinary scene, attend one of the many food festivals and markets held throughout the state. These lively events offer an opportunity to taste a variety of local dishes, sample artisanal products, and connect with the passionate chefs, bakers, and producers behind the flavors.

Supporting Local Producers

By enjoying Indiana's local food and beverages, you contribute to the vitality of the state's culinary community. Your support not only sustains local businesses but also fosters a sense of pride and appreciation for the rich gastronomic heritage of the Hoosier State.

As you savor the tastes of Indiana, each dish and beverage becomes a unique memory, weaving the tapestry of your culinary journey through this vibrant and flavorful region.

Take home the flavors of Indiana with locally produced food and beverages. Pack your bags with jars of artisanal jams, bottles of locally brewed beer, or bags of freshly roasted coffee.

Explore antique stores along Indiana's Antique Alley to find vintage souvenirs that harken back to the state's earlier years. Collect antique postcards, retro travel brochures, or vintage memorabilia.

Handmade Jewelry

Handmade Jewelry: Indiana's Artistic Adornments

Nature-Inspired Designs

Indiana's natural beauty serves as a wellspring of inspiration for handmade jewelry artists. Admire necklaces and earrings featuring delicate leaves, flowers, and vines, intricately crafted to capture the essence of Indiana's lush forests and vibrant flora. Each piece embodies the tranquility and wonder of the state's natural landscapes.

Gemstones and Minerals

Jewelry artists often incorporate locally sourced gemstones and minerals into their creations, highlighting the geological diversity of Indiana. From luminous geodes and agates to vibrant jasper and calcite, these gemstones become centerpieces of unique and captivating jewelry pieces.

Symbols of Heritage

Handmade jewelry in Indiana often celebrates the state's cultural heritage through symbolic designs. Look for pieces adorned with motifs representing Native American traditions, Amish craftsmanship, and the state's historical landmarks. These symbols carry the stories of Indiana's past, keeping its heritage alive in wearable art.

Artistry in Metals

Explore jewelry crafted from various metals, showcasing the artistry of Indiana's skilled metalsmiths. From sterling silver pendants etched with intricate designs to copper bracelets displaying rustic charm, each piece reflects the craftsmanship and creativity of the artists who shape them.

Hand-Stamped Jewelry

One of the popular trends in handmade jewelry is hand-stamped pieces that can be customized with names, dates, or meaningful phrases. Personalize your jewelry with the coordinates of your favorite Indiana destination, the initials of loved ones, or a heartfelt message that holds significance to you.

Beaded Creations
Beaded jewelry reveals a kaleidoscope of colors and textures, reflecting the artistic diversity of Indiana's jewelry makers. Admire bracelets adorned with sparkling beads, statement necklaces featuring a fusion of gemstones and glass beads, and earrings that dance with every movement.

Honoring Indiana's Sports Teams
For sports enthusiasts, handmade jewelry pays tribute to Indiana's beloved sports teams. Find bracelets and necklaces adorned with team colors and logos, allowing you to carry your team spirit with you wherever you go.

Whether you seek a nature-inspired pendant, a gemstone ring, or a symbolic bracelet, each piece of handmade jewelry becomes a wearable work of art—a testament to the talent, passion, and creativity of Indiana's artisans.

Supporting Local Artisans
By choosing handmade jewelry, you support local artisans and their dedication to their craft. The purchase of these unique pieces not only adds beauty to your jewelry collection but also fosters a sense of community and appreciation for the artistry that thrives in the Hoosier State.

As you explore the world of handmade jewelry in Indiana, each piece you select becomes more than an accessory; it becomes a cherished reminder of the state's artistic soul and the talented hands that shape its adornments.

Discover unique jewelry pieces created by local artisans, featuring gemstones, metals, and designs inspired by Indiana's natural beauty and cultural heritage.

Vintage Souvenirs

Vintage Souvenirs: Unearthing Indiana's Nostalgic Treasures

Antique Postcards

Among the delightful vintage souvenirs, antique postcards stand out as windows to Indiana's past. These beautifully illustrated postcards depict historic landmarks, scenic vistas, and bustling cities of a bygone era. As you collect these postcards, you'll journey back in time to witness the state's evolution and see how it has retained its allure throughout the years.

Retro Travel Brochures

Retro travel brochures add a touch of old-world charm to your collection of vintage souvenirs. These printed gems once enticed travelers to explore Indiana's attractions and events. With their colorful graphics and captivating descriptions, they provide a glimpse into the excitement and wonder that travelers experienced in years past.

Vintage Memorabilia

Indiana's rich history is beautifully preserved in vintage memorabilia. Collectible items such as pins, badges, and buttons from state fairs, festivals, and historic events offer a tangible connection to Indiana's cultural heritage. Each piece of vintage memorabilia carries the stories of the past, becoming a cherished addition to your treasure trove of Indiana souvenirs.

Historical Artifacts

Embark on a treasure hunt for historical artifacts, which range from antique maps and prints to vintage books and documents. Discover the stories of Indiana's early settlers, the growth of its cities, and the cultural milestones that shaped the state's identity. These artifacts provide a glimpse into the past and deepen your appreciation for Indiana's unique heritage.

Collectible Coins and Tokens

For numismatic enthusiasts, collectible coins and tokens offer a fascinating glimpse into Indiana's past commerce and history. Seek out coins minted during important events or tokens issued by local businesses of days gone by. Each coin and token is a small piece of Indiana's story, waiting to be unearthed and appreciated.

Commemorative Plates and Souvenir Spoons

Vintage commemorative plates and souvenir spoons showcase the artistic craftsmanship of yesteryears. These decorative items often feature iconic landmarks, historical figures, or notable events in Indiana's history. Displaying these plates and spoons adds a touch of elegance to your collection and serves as a reminder of the state's cultural significance.

Exploring Antique Stores

Uncover the hidden gems of Indiana's vintage souvenirs by exploring antique stores and markets. These treasure troves are havens for collectors and history enthusiasts, offering a wide array of authentic items that hold the charm of a bygone era. Whether you stumble upon a unique postcard, a rare coin, or a captivating brochure, each find tells a tale of Indiana's past waiting to be cherished anew.

Collecting vintage souvenirs is not just a hobby; it's a way to connect with the essence of Indiana's history, culture, and heritage. As you add these nostalgic treasures to your collection, they become more than mere objects; they become portals to the rich tapestry of Indiana's past.

Conclusion: A Journey to Remember

As your adventure through Indiana concludes, you'll carry with you a treasure trove of memories and experiences. From the iconic sights of Indianapolis to the serene landscapes of state parks, Indiana offers a diverse array of attractions for every traveler.

You've explored the rich history, embraced the arts and culture, tasted delectable cuisines, and embarked on exciting adventures. Whether you're a history buff, a nature lover, a sports enthusiast, or a foodie, Indiana has woven its magic into your heart.

Remember that Indiana's charm extends beyond its attractions; it lies in the warmth and hospitality of its people—the genuine Hoosier spirit. As you bid farewell to the Crossroads of America, know that you can always return to uncover more of its hidden wonders.

May the memories you've created and the stories you've gathered during your time in Indiana inspire you to embark on further journeys and embrace the beauty of the world.

Safe travels, and until we meet again, farewell!

if you have any other requests, feel free to let me know. Safe travels!

7-Day indiana Itinerary

Creating a 7-day itinerary for Indiana allows you to explore a variety of attractions and experiences in the state. Indiana offers a mix of natural beauty, history, culture, and outdoor activities. Here's a sample itinerary for your 7-day trip:

Day 1: Arrival in Indianapolis

Arrive in Indianapolis, the capital city of Indiana.

Check into your hotel and freshen up.

Visit the Indianapolis Museum of Art or the Newfields, which features a beautiful art collection and gardens.

Explore the downtown area, including Monument Circle, where you can see the Soldiers and Sailors Monument.

Enjoy dinner at a local restaurant in the downtown area.

Day 2: Indianapolis

Begin your day with a visit to the Indianapolis Motor Speedway, home to the famous Indy 500 race.

Tour the Indianapolis Motor Speedway Museum.

In the afternoon, visit the Indianapolis Zoo or the Children's Museum of Indianapolis, depending on your interests.

Have dinner at a local brewery or restaurant.

Day 3: Bloomington

Drive to Bloomington, home to Indiana University.

Explore the beautiful campus and enjoy lunch in the college town atmosphere.

Visit the Tibetan Mongolian Buddhist Cultural Center for a unique cultural experience.

Hike or take a nature walk in nearby Hoosier National Forest.

Return to Bloomington for dinner and relaxation.

Day 4: French Lick and West Baden Springs

Drive to French Lick, a historic resort town in southern Indiana.

Tour the French Lick Springs Hotel and the West Baden Springs Hotel, both of which are architectural gems.

Visit the French Lick Casino for some entertainment.

Enjoy dinner at one of the resort's fine dining options.

Day 5: Brown County

Drive to Brown County, known as the "Little Smokies" due to its scenic beauty.

Explore the charming town of Nashville, known for its art galleries and unique shops.

Take a hike in Brown County State Park, which offers numerous trails and beautiful vistas.

Enjoy dinner at a local restaurant in Nashville.

Day 6: South Bend

Drive to South Bend, home to the University of Notre Dame.

Visit the campus of Notre Dame and the historic Basilica of the Sacred Heart.

Explore the Studebaker National Museum for a look at the history of automobiles.

Have dinner in downtown South Bend.

Day 7: Lake Michigan and Departure

Drive to the Indiana Dunes National Park on the shores of Lake Michigan.

Spend the morning hiking and exploring the sand dunes, beaches, and trails.

Have a picnic lunch at the park.

In the afternoon, head back to Indianapolis for your departure.

This itinerary offers a mix of cultural, natural, and historical experiences in Indiana. Of course, you can adjust it based on your interests and the specific activities or attractions you want to prioritize. Indiana has much more to offer, so consider extending your stay or making additional stops if you have the time.

Helpful Websites and Resources for Traveling in indiana

When planning a trip to Indiana, it's helpful to have access to various websites and resources that can provide you with information on attractions, accommodations, dining options, and more. Here are some helpful websites and resources for traveling in Indiana:

VisitIndiana.com: The official website of the Indiana Office of Tourism Development, offering a comprehensive guide to attractions, events, accommodations, and travel tips across the state.

Indiana Dunes Tourism: If you plan to visit the Indiana Dunes, their website provides information on the national park, local activities, and lodging options.

Indiana State Parks: The Indiana Department of Natural Resources has a website dedicated to Indiana's state parks and reservoirs, providing details on hiking trails, camping, and recreational activities.

Historic Indiana: Discover the state's historical attractions, including museums, landmarks, and heritage sites, on this resourceful website.

TripAdvisor Indiana: TripAdvisor is a valuable resource for traveler reviews, ratings, and recommendations for hotels, restaurants, and attractions in Indiana.

Yelp Indiana: Similar to TripAdvisor, Yelp offers reviews and ratings for dining, shopping, and entertainment options throughout the state.

Indiana Foodways Alliance: If you're a food enthusiast, this website highlights Indiana's culinary culture, including the Hoosier Pie Trail and other food-related adventures.

Indiana Wineries and Breweries: Explore the state's wineries and craft breweries by visiting the Indiana Wine Grape Council and the Brewers of Indiana Guild websites.

Indiana Department of Transportation: For road trip planning and current road conditions, check the Indiana DOT website for maps, traffic updates, and construction alerts.

Indiana Events Calendar: Stay up-to-date on local events, festivals, and happenings by consulting Indiana event calendars such as Eventbrite, Indiana Festivals, and local event websites for specific cities or regions.

Indiana Travel Forums: Websites like IndianaTalks.com or travel-related subreddits can be great places to ask questions and get recommendations from fellow travelers.

Indiana State Tourism Social Media: Follow Indiana's official tourism social media accounts on platforms like Instagram, Facebook, and Twitter for inspiration and real-time updates.

Indiana Historical Society: For history buffs, the Indiana Historical Society website offers resources on historical sites, genealogy, and research opportunities.

Indiana Official Roadway Map: Download or request a physical copy of the Indiana Official

Roadway Map from the Indiana Department of Transportation for navigation and trip planning.

Local Tourism Bureaus: Many cities and regions within Indiana have their own tourism bureaus or chambers of commerce websites that provide localized information and recommendations.

Remember to check for the most up-to-date information and resources as your travel dates approach. These websites should help you plan a memorable trip to the Hoosier State.

Tourist-Friendly Apps to Download for Your Trip to indiana

When traveling to Indiana, having the right apps on your smartphone can enhance your experience and make your trip more enjoyable. Here are some tourist-friendly apps to consider downloading for your trip to Indiana:

1. Visit Indiana (Official Indiana Travel Guide):
iOS: Visit Indiana on the App Store
Android: Visit Indiana on Google Play

The official app of the Indiana Office of Tourism Development provides information on attractions, events, accommodations, and dining options across the state.

2. Google Maps:

iOS: Google Maps on the App Store

Android: Google Maps on Google Play

Google Maps is a must-have for navigation, real-time traffic updates, and finding nearby restaurants, gas stations, and attractions.

3. Yelp:

iOS: Yelp on the App Store

Android: Yelp on Google Play

Use Yelp to discover reviews and ratings for dining, shopping, and entertainment options throughout Indiana.

4. TripAdvisor:

iOS: TripAdvisor on the App Store

Android: TripAdvisor on Google Play

TripAdvisor provides traveler reviews, ratings, and recommendations for hotels, restaurants, and attractions in Indiana.

5. Airbnb:

iOS: Airbnb on the App Store

Android: Airbnb on Google Play

If you plan to book vacation rentals or unique accommodations, Airbnb's app can be convenient.

6. Uber/Lyft:

iOS (Uber): Uber on the App Store

Android (Uber): Uber on Google Play

iOS (Lyft): Lyft on the App Store

Android (Lyft): Lyft on Google Play

Ride-sharing apps like Uber and Lyft are handy for getting around in cities like Indianapolis.

7. GasBuddy:

iOS: GasBuddy on the App Store

Android: GasBuddy on Google Play

GasBuddy helps you find the cheapest gas prices in your area while traveling.

8. Roadtrippers:

iOS: Roadtrippers on the App Store

Android: Roadtrippers on Google Play

Roadtrippers is ideal for planning road trips, discovering attractions, and creating itineraries.

9. Weather Apps:

Check your preferred weather app (e.g., The Weather Channel, Weather Underground, or your device's built-in weather app) to stay updated on weather conditions during your trip.

10. Indiana State Parks and Reservoirs Apps:

- Some of Indiana's state parks and reservoirs may have their own apps with trail maps and park-specific information. Check the app store for relevant options.

Make sure to download these apps before your trip to have access to information and services while on the go in Indiana.

FINAL THOUGHT ON INDIANA

Indiana is a diverse and inviting state with much to offer travelers. From the vibrant city life of Indianapolis to the natural beauty of the Indiana Dunes, and from the rich history of French Lick to the small-town charm of places like Nashville and Bloomington, Indiana has something for everyone.

Here are some final thoughts on Indiana:
Cultural Richness: Indiana's cultural scene is thriving. Whether you're interested in art, history, sports, or music, you'll find plenty of opportunities to explore and enjoy.

Outdoor Adventures: The state boasts numerous outdoor attractions, including state parks, forests, lakes, and hiking trails. Indiana Dunes National Park, in particular, offers a unique blend of sand dunes and Lake Michigan shoreline.

Sports Enthusiasts: Indiana is a sports lover's paradise. It's home to the Indianapolis 500, the Indianapolis Colts, and the NCAA Hall of Champions, making it a great destination for sports enthusiasts.

Hoosier Hospitality: Hoosiers are known for their friendly and welcoming nature. You'll likely encounter warm hospitality and helpful locals during your visit.

Historic Landmarks: Explore historical sites such as the French Lick Springs Hotel, West Baden Springs Hotel, and the many museums and monuments that showcase Indiana's past.

Culinary Delights: Don't miss the opportunity to sample Indiana's culinary offerings, including local farm-to-table restaurants and classic Hoosier dishes like breaded pork tenderloin sandwiches.

Scenic Drives: Indiana offers scenic drives, particularly during the fall when the foliage transforms into a beautiful array of colors. Brown County is known for its picturesque drives.

Educational Opportunities: If you're interested in learning more about history, science, or culture, Indiana has excellent museums and educational institutions to visit.

In conclusion, Indiana is a state that often surprises visitors with its diversity and charm. Whether you're exploring its cities, enjoying its natural beauty, or immersing yourself in its history and culture, you're likely to find something that captures your interest and makes your trip to Indiana memorable.

Made in United States
North Haven, CT
26 November 2023

44577864R00098